This Sickness We Call Love

By:

Violette L. Meier

VIORI PUBLISHING

Viori Publishing
P.O. Box 5283
Atlanta, GA 31107

This book is a work of fiction. The characters and events portrayed in this book are products of the author's imagination. Any similarity to real persons, living or dead, business establishments, events or locals is coincidental and not intended by the author.

ISBN: 978-0-9887805-3-8

Printed in the United States of America

Cover and Interior Designed by Viori Publishing

DEDICATED

... to all who broke my heart.
.... to my love Ari who put it back together again.

ACKNOWLEDGEMENT

I would like to thank God for blessing me. I give special thanks to my family and the most wonderful children in creation (Xoe, Zahyir, Ruah, Aura, Kiera, & Arman). I thank my wonderful mother who is the rock of my family and my sisters and brothers (Vernard, Valerie, Velma, & Sonny) for always supporting me. Thanks to all my friends and to all who believe in me. I am eternally grateful.

I WILL LIVE!
I will weep with the wind
So my tears will blow away
Carrying this sorrow far away from me
Life is but a fast writing pen
Producing poetry until the ink runs thin
I will be that song upon paper personified
A living testimony of bleeding heart
I will live each day worshipping freedom
Bowing to the God of all
Who gave me this life to dance
To prance around in glory
To be the novel
To live the movie
I will laugh until my lungs collapse
And relapse into spirit
And flee from this earthly space

MIND GAMES

So much time wasted on others when from day one
Butterflies fluttered within me when you are near me
Why couldn't my heart yell "hear me!"
To my body determined to ignore the feelings I was destined for
Countless times I've closed my eyes and wondered what could have been
But didn't become
What is the sum of this twisted equation
That lazily works on my brain like advanced trigonometry on occasion
Too little too late I contemplate about what if you and me became WE
But I guess WE weren't in the cards you see
Maybe destiny enjoys playing cruel jokes
But I still win again and again when you visit my dreams
In a future that seems more logically real regarding the future of us
In my heart you will always be mine
Maybe next lifetime we will speak up and not let time sneak up
And extinguish a spark destined to grow into an immense inferno
Woulda, coulda, shoulda only exists in memory's kiss
Ever so often blessing me with this sweet sensation of idealized revelations
Please release me from your hypnotic trance

(cont...)

That forces my heart to dance every time you lay
eyes on me
You see, this power you have over me
Grows stronger the longer I am in your presence
And seems to last an eternity
I guess that will forever be you and me.

MUST END

Delicate fingers trace my lips
Hot kisses peck my face
Your eyes closed shut
The silence says so much

You love me

A deep breath you take
Words forced back in your throat
Squeeze tight my body
So close – skin to skin
Pores sucking on one another
Meshed into one flesh
Lips touch soft then quick
Swept up in the moment
Attacking tongues then flailing arms
Gripping, groping, grabbing
Legs locked tight around your back

I love you too

Hearts racing like stallions
Limbs quaking
All the love we're making must end

A FEAST OF HEART

I sit before you
a feast of heart
plated and pumping in lamentation.
Blood sauce to sweeten your lips.
My love muscle palpitates
anticipating the cut of your teeth.
Here I am.
Raw.
Oh! Naked! Raw!
Uncovered and bearing no shame.
Yet my offering,
Bread and wine
Flesh and blood
Unholy communion
Offering up my mortality,
go untouched .
I beg you to
consume my life
kiss away death
drink down my sorrow
chew up my pain savor my bitterness
swallow and be filled
then
please love me!

DREAM LOVER

His raven hair flows through my fingers.
Lip to lip we lock --
tongues flickering like serpents sniffing.
"Usted es hermosa," he whispers while massaging
my torso
with his full pecan lips.
I shiver from toe to finger tip.
His eyes penetrate mine –
brown like sand dunes.
Cloud nine!!!
My womanhood is in full bloom.
"Exhale," he commands with his strong hands.
I do--
my face light blue—
a child anew.
"Jardin de juegos," he whispers as his fingers
start to go and conquer and divide.
My blood pressure an amusement ride.
"Es mi deseo darle placer ."
I am transported into deepest ardor.
I awake!
My Latin lover is no more.

HUSBAND

When you place your lips upon me
My heart beats like the thundering drums of Africa
Echoing through my torso –
A hollow shell – empty
Save for this heart
Reaching through foreign ancestry
To grab the lustier creature lurking inside of me
I meditate on your stature – strong.
I crave you.
Not just physical beauty but the mental intricate
workings
Of your cerebral artistry
Your soul sings
Like the erotic serenade of crickets
Seeking companionship in the thicket of lush green
You grace me with your being.
Standing upright eclipsing my eyes like
Sun and moon embracing in the shadow
Defacing my previous preconceived fantasies
That falls short of thee
How many times can I lose myself within your
caress?
And savor each intimate tryst that sparks and glint
Like a firefly kiss that ignites with pure chemistry
Creating a chaotic emotional symphony
Bringing envy to mythical Eros
Yet represents our reality
Sweet man of mine
Lay thy hand upon my quivering cheek
Folding under your touch like a forlorn rose

(cont...)

Upon its last petal weak
As feeble as an angel falling with wounded wing
I realize how blessed I am among women
To live this fervent dream of lovers resurrecting
magic
Each morning with a mere kiss
And each night in pure bliss
I long for eternity my ebony prince
Please grant me this.

LOVE

Love is
you and I, my heart
holding hands
knuckles white as we cling together grasping
air tight fists holding on through
melancholy disappointments
and eternal struggles tearing away
at our flesh.
Yet we hold on
hand in hand like glued puzzle pieces.
The winds of despair blow hard against us
as one body flaps through the wind.
The other grows stronger
biceps bulging -triceps straining
pulling threefold
using every bit of body, mind, and soul
until we are both standing
fingers locked and feet firm
readying ourselves for the next challenger
beckoning war.
Who will it be
wearing impregnable armor
carrying a battering ram
ready to knock us apart
forcing one of us to watch as the other
floats off into oblivion?
The warrior – hardships
come blazing with banners snapping in the harsh
breeze.
Yet we stand and sometimes fall

(cont.)

knees bruised by jagged ground
arms tired and hands swollen.
Yet we cling.
Our love is all we have.
All we are
and
all we will ever be.

UNFULFILLED

Echoing emptiness ricochet through my fleshy shell
Bouncing into everlasting purposelessness
Fruitlessly trying to fill the hole with nothingness
Constantly producing tears, pitiful moans
Staring out from hopeless eyes
Reaching through dormant hands
Hands that toil for no task
Inhaling despair
Exhaling forsaken dreams
Sleeping through opportunities
Fearing change
Dodging chance
Welcoming failure with pious stupidity
Yearning to be miraculously filled
Yet lazily accepting the bland monotony of
mediocrity
Swallowing more empty
Gorging on average
Forgetting to live free

DEPRIVED

These crazy cravings of carnal crassness crawl through my flesh corrupting my soul with lusty longings of loving relations.
Oh why fill this emptiness of wanting to be loved with hollow desire delicately dancing upon my sacred delights.
I do not want anyone but you.
Yet the coldness in your stare wears me down to bone and dust.
I'm not deserving of the passionless pouts of your kissless lips that leave mine dry and untouched.
What am I to do, my love, when my passes are deemed less than a stingless bee perched upon the sweetness of your cocoa?
Don't go on with the heatless greetings that trickle from your uninterested lips into my yearning ears begging for the words that won't come forth from your mouth.
I lay here silently wishing—missing what we once were.
Then these crazy cravings come condemning me to eternal damnation.
I'm dreading the sudden death occasion when you will banish them forever more by reassuring me that you love me and always will.

MY MC
He sits on a rock in the midst of Central Park
as the skyscrapers peer over his shoulder hoping for
a glimpse of his words
He palms a pad in one hand as the other spills ink
upon paper absorbing true lyrics of poetic
phenomena
I see his lips humming the beat that drums through
his brain
as his head nods and feet beat against concrete
An MC
with vivid visions of microphone victories
galloping through his psyche
lyrically crushing those who dare to contend
against the might of his tongue and pen
He sits
heart pumping against his shirt
The hurt of the world mingling with birds singing
as his page flips
and those juicy lips leak poetic poison
drowning within the noise of the city

I ALMOST FORGOT MY DIVINITY

I allowed you to pull me down
into primordial cesspools of victimhood
Oh! I bowed down to an ideal -
carnal idolatry
Babylonian harlotry
Girding my loins in withering violets
Tossing my perfumed palms to the dust
just to be next to you
my unholy monarch
So blinded by my own imagination
Looking upon you with veiled awe
Valentines for eyes
I stare breathless
Heart quaking with joy
Joy of having one so sacred in my midst
But
The veil dropped
and you were no longer god but fiend
dirty and muddied in your own deceit
And I
stupefied and confused
Not by you
but by the images I painted
with hopeful brushes and fanciful inks
The prostrate position I had taken
lips kissing your juicy heels
lapping the bloody wine as your toes squish my heart
Oh! The horror
The unmitigated gall
To think!
I almost forgot my divinity

AWKWARD HEART RHYME

You say you have no time
No time for you and me
Yet you touch me
Stir my soul within
Shake everything I believe in
When your arms are surrounding me
Your eyes seem happy to see
Your hands to touch
Your lips to kiss
Your arms to hold
Your heart to share
Yet there is no future you say
Our demise is only months away
We talk for hours on end
Like lovers...like equals...like friends
Yet you compartmentalize
Placing me in a box half my size
And file me away
We make love grasping hands
Moaning in pleasure
Rolling like thunder
Laughing like children
Climaxing in wonder
Yet it's only a matter of time you say
That all this we have will fade away
For the truth stands that we are not free
You have your work
My life is filled with responsibilities
Which crush the hopes of you and me
Now I don't know if I agree

(cont...)

If you're right or wrong
I'll wait and see
For nothing in this life is by chance
So I'll wait...I'll enjoy
I'll like...I'll love
I'll dream...I'll dance
I'll hope...I'll pray
I'll think of you everyday
And maybe...just maybe
Time will be nothing between you and me
The future will hold infinite possibilities
Your heart will open
Your file system broken
My life will change accordingly
And we'll simply be!

PASSIONATELY FLAVORFUL

The first time you bit into my apple
Your tongue lapping up sweetness
Juice glossing your lips
As you flicked my seed
And parted the meat and skin
I withered beneath you
I savored you savoring me
My mouth parted to taste your goodness
Melted around your stiffened stem
Suckled the flavorful fullness
That rested between my gentle teeth
With happy kisses
With joyful licks
I tried to swallow you whole
You tasting me
I tasting you
So sweet
So ***passionately flavorful***!

NO WAILING

Across the bed I lay
Heart thumping in my neck
Breathing labored
Head swollen with thoughts
I want to cry
But can't
My desire is to weep until my eyes bleed
Until my skin corrodes
Become weathered by acid tears
But I remain soft flesh
Whole and free
No tears
No wailing for me!

YOUR DANCE

So skillful – your moves
Smooth, light, quick
As you tap dance all over my heart,
Are you even aware that you are killing me with
every kick?
Can you feel my organ squish under your heel?
It gushes between your toes?
When I say, "I love you."
Oh! How fast your foot goes!
The beat begins when I can't stop thinking of you.
Your fingers snap; your hands clap.
You give me a spin then your thighs a slap.
With an, "I miss you."
You grind my flesh into the concrete.
I ask to see you.
You jump, wiggle your hips and shuffle your feet.
Do you even see the scarlet prints you leave
Trailing around town?
Does the wetness of my heart excite you
As your feet touch the ground?
It must be nice to dance so easy.
Not a care or a second thought.
To glide across the floor so quickly.
Churning my heart into salt.

REAL LOVE POEM

The newness is gone
the crisp corners
the first juicy bite
the nervous queasiness
when I first looked at you
Now comfort has set in
like our old sofa
perfectly molding around us
as we fit into one another
like measuring cups stacked
and watch the glory of Hollywood
parade across our TV screen
Your hands are as familiar as my own
They drift across my body barely noticed
like a wisp of cloud almost thin
enough not to be seen
When I look into your face my heart does not race
but engage in a slow and steady gallop
Your handsomeness is still extreme but not as
potent
I can now handle the dose
I have become immune from my millionth stare
I've seen you unshaven with crust cornered eyes
and foul breath
Yet something in the grossness of your humanity
brings me ever so much closer to eternity beside you
What we share is genuine-unique-one of a kind
built to endure drops, spills, tears, and scrapes
evolving and mutating into homogenous harmony
We are the fit who survive-like roaches

(cont.)

Forever and ever
You and I
Love
Real love
True love
love

I CAN'T MAKE YOU LOVE ME

There is nothing I can do
I contemplate scarlet undies
Fuzzy heels
Upswept hair
But there is nothing sexy I can possibly wear
or offer to win your heart
my arms can't squeeze tight enough
my lips hungry enough
my breasts firm enough
my hips fast enough
my talents aren't good enough
to capture the essence of you
my mind is not sharp enough
no matter my IQ
my education
my common sense
my logical rationings
I can't think of a way to win you
To woo you
To entice you
My money isn't enough
My coffer is bare
My bank account low
My potential won't do
No matter how great my promise is
I just can't make you love me
If you don't want to

OVER?

I can still feel your heartbeat
Quick then miraculously slowed
You sink into calm
A feathery snore ruffles your nose
I smile
The smell of you comforts me
Your skin inhumanly soft
My eyes close
I am at peace
So short lived was this moment
Snatched away quicker than it started
I tear
Memories not really formed
The wound is too fresh
Is it over?

CRAVINGS

I crave you like chocolate covered almonds at
midnight
Silky against my tongue
Your name falls
And I swallow
Greedily inhale the thought of you
Digesting your toothsome essence
If only I could have you now
Close to me
Touching what prays to be touched
Only the way you can
Unfolding the inner me
Laying wide in juicy slices
Waiting to be devoured
By delicate lips and miraculous tongue
Oh I can feel you
Hard...deep...strong
I close my eyes
Brace myself for delicious pain
Readying my mouth to belt your name
Yet again...
The disappointment is the same
You are not here
My hunger rages on
I'm left alone
Craving once again

MUST I LEAVE THIS ROOM?

You sit near your windowsill
Beer in hand
Cigarette in mouth
Smoke floating from your nose encircling your head
like a halo
The moon illuminating your sienna skin
Soft skin gleaming with perspiration
Glowing from the dew of our love making
I lay across your bed and stare
As a child fascinated by what's new
I listen to every word
Every syllable shaped by your mouth
Your voice so masculine yet tender
Tenor tone – meek but viral and strong
Speaking notes so sweet
I stare and am jubilant to be here
You tell me of past pains
Family matters and financial gain
You speak of business ventures
And aspirations magnifying your full potential
I am silenced by the mystery in your eyes
Attracted by the enigma of you
It dawns on me after all these years
That I never truly knew who you were
The man who you have become
The man you want to be
The man you wish to avoid
A sigh escapes my lips
My heart pauses then begins again
Epiphany!

(cont...)

Angels descend upon me
One whispers to enlighten me
And I realize that there is a possibility that you were
made for me
You and I truly are meant to be more than the world
imagined
Really real
Really true
Really happy
I smile at you and you look at me
Confused
Confused about my awkward smirk
Smirk widening my eyes
Twisting my mouth upward
You ask what's wrong with me
Why I'm looking at you like that
I laugh and lay back
Tell you you'll never be rid of me
Fall onto your firm mattress
Catching me with armless arms
My soul is warmed
Until I hear my alarm sound
My feet are placed back on the ground
And reality sets in
Outside this room the world will be cold once again
Outside this momentary paradise Hades sits as
biting as ice
Real life
My life

(cont…)

Your life
No life
I want to weep
I desire to cry for you and I
For we are only a moment lost in time
Which must end eventually
But why? Why?
WHY!
Why must I leave this room…

WRETCHED
Flesh pulsating with pining
Drunken by physical wanting
I fall upon knees
Knees trembling with spent desire
Aching with ungodly passion
Unashamed of my sins
Reminiscing on each thrust
My belly flutters
My loins twinge
Yet guilt is blocked out of mind
Buried beneath immediate gratification
So wretched am I
Day dreaming of the next time I can be defiled
Hoping for a moment of frantic fondling
Praying for profane intensity
Yet I damn myself
Why hasn't guilt come to condemn?
Why is my conscious so clear?
So cold? So calculated?
So wretched?
Where is the fear? The pain? The confusion?
My soul accepts sin as natural
It exclaims with excitement
The excellence in enthusiastic lust making
Wretched
So wretched
Oh so wretched I have become!
Joy in sinfully sensual repetition
Addicted to the idea of what's new
Of what's you

FOOLISH

What am I doing?
Tumbling over obvious rocks purposely

Screaming on a roller coaster alone
Excitement morphing to fear
Yet I keep getting on
Letting the bar halt my circulation
Willingly tossed until neck strains in warranted pain

Consciously choosing plastic over diamonds
Gloom before glitter

Grasping at the ocean floor
Opening mouth for water to invade
Inhaling to expedite suffocation

Foolish, foolish me
Drawn to destruction
Adoring aching

Blindfolded and falling upon bloody knees
Knees boiling with blisters
But blissful in blindness
Fingers refusing to fondle the fold

Oh so foolish
Foolish me

FLATTER ME just for a moment
Allow me to dream
Dream of you and I
Skipping in the sunshine
Dancing in day light
Bold and unapologetic
Escaping the night
Throwing our cloaks to the wind
Birthing flame to wicks
Allowing the brightness to flow in
Avoiding secret
Souls naked as jay birds
Bare for all to see
Smiles as wide as Cheshire cats
Laughter too high to be heard
Just flatter me
Pretend it could be real
Converting illicit to legit
Ignoring the world
Living what we feel
The vastness of eternity
Encompassing only you and me
Oh how exhilarating fiction can be
If you would just flatter me
Imagine freedom
Unadulterated delight
Breaking free of darkness
Bathing in the light
No more private meetings
No more late night trysts
Right out in the open
Spot lights illuminating each kiss
Oh just flatter me!

BOY PLEASE SET ME FREE
Once lashing tongues
Now crashing tongues
Hooked within wanting mouths
Forever hating you
Now dating you
Lord, tell me how!
Brimstone and fire
Melts into passion and desire
What has become of me?
Cringing chin
Now tingling skin
Boy please set me free!

ASHAMED

My God frowns upon me
Righteousness lost
Another angel's wings ripped away
My hypocrisy heckles me
Destiny cloudy
I break my vows and refuse to look in the mirror
I've become the person I hate most
I love
Oh I love
But
I'm tired
So very tired
Is that an excuse to be so
Infatuated
Infuriated
Inebriated
In love with you?
Tears drown my shame
I no longer know my name
Yet
I still want you

STRUGGLE
It pens down my tongue
Presses hard against my teeth
Tries to force my mouth ajar
But I swallow
It is held at bay
Again
It bounces against my cheeks
Swings from my tonsils
Swells my insides
Pushes the air from my lungs
I inhale
Hold my breath
Calm it down
Yet again
It tickles the back of my throat
Scratches at the roof of my mouth
Burns within my heart
Seeps through my teeth
I give up
I set it free
"I love you"

UNWORTHY
I lay nude before you
Bearing every inch of me
I unfold my innocence
Expose my shame
Present to you my heart...glimmers of my soul
Yet
No response
My pride cowers in corners
My love a gift to be gained
I speak out in faith
I tell you how my stomach flutters
How my life has changed
How my mind prays your name
Yet
No response
No welcome or rejection
No agreement or determent
Nothing
You deem me unworthy of your response

KISSING YOU

Oh let me drink your lips
Suck the juicy sweetness of its softness
I taste your tongue as my tongue tangos with it
Twisting as breaths escape in hurried gusts
Your hands upon me
Oh your hands
Hands that curl my skin with each stroke
My neck welcomes your lips
It melts under each warm peck
Tickled by wanton whiskers as your mouth ravishes
me
My shoulders drop in submission
Anxious for their turn to be pecked
Begging for your lips to take them
And cover them in satin snuggles
Now my breasts leap with desire
They rise to meet your greeting
Areolas stiffen into pulsating peaks
Who swell with anticipation of your suckling
sensations
Again let me sip your lips
Take one more swig before you delve into me
Just one more
One more soft smooch before I am taken
Taken into all that is me
Welcoming you
Inside

PERPETUAL CHILDREN

here we are
perpetual children
lost—very lost and astray
we bounce around
laughing and crying simultaneously
building bombs and daring them to explode
defiling our bodies
toying with emotions
fantasizing about slitting wrists during orgasm
screaming for mercy while inflicting pain
we crawl on all fours
no dignity or shame
nameless faceless blameless
children
teetering between damnation and salvation daily
praying with fingers crossed
dancing the dance of the lost
we kick and twirl
hoping to leave this world with purpose
yet we know this may never occur
so we whirl and whirl around
jumping up and falling down
praying to be seen
look at me! look at me!
see me!
admire me!
acknowledge me!
please

(cont...)

love me!
please love me!
attention is what we breath
if God will not answer
we will continue to scream
love me! Show me!
before I destroy everything just to be noticed
by
you

I ACHE
The pain itself throbs
Vibrates within my core
A dark vacuum of rot
Chipping and flaking
Darkening by the second
A worm hole in my heart
Constantly chewed upon with spiked teeth
Teeth without mouth
Mouth without head
Just invisible demons
Gnawing on my perverse nature
I ache
Yes, I hurt
The pain drowns within itself
Swallowed and digested
Rebirthed to hurt again
Wet, slimy, grimy, gray
Like a dust covered booger
It sticks to my ribs
Resident evil—daring eviction
It's acidy goo eating each artery
I ache
My heart hurts!
As though no body carries it
It carelessly pounds
Pumping sickening sorrow through my blood stream
Icky nothingness
Disappointing disaster
Predictable chaos
I ache

(cont...)

I hurt
Yet
I can't cry
My eyes – deserts
In drought—Sand filled, salty, empty wells
Look deep and see the pit
That leads to my broken heart.

FLAT LINING
I loved you
As Gilgamesh did Enkidu
I would've traveled beyond the end of the earth
Just to revive you
But...
It seems as if your pulse is still weak
Fading and nearly still
When it comes to me
You have lost your will to live
You rather pass away to the unknown
Than to dwell in our home
Where a decade has built our twin thrones
Once upon a time you would have stolen fire from
the gods
Just to ignite my failing heart
If the land of shade summoned me
You would've threatened the Witch of Endor
Forced her to use her dark charms
To bring me back from Sheol into your arms
Now if I perish I perish
If you die you die
The passion has left us both
Passion-our life fuel- is flat lining

LOVE ME

Oh beautiful man of mine
who's eyes are like thousands of stars
intertwined together into two holy clusters peering
into my heart.
You are the one!
Oh one of many fascinating smiles
owner of petal soft lips that drive my soul wild
leaping with flames causing my being to dance in a
frenzied trance every time I spy those teeth!
Ebony Manitou –deity of my blues—my joys—my
gay coy arms that long for you!
Sweet thing of my dreams who has blessed my
reality with your physical being.
Don't you see that breath only enters me for only
one reason—to be yours so…
Please love me!

NEAR
To be near you
Drunken by your scent
Intoxicated by the moistness of your lips
Your shoulders as wide as boulders
My hips ache with dreams of you
Your hands
Oh, your hands
Dark and determined to devour
Deflower
Overpower me
My heart flutters
Beats
Bangs
Cries out
The anticipation overwhelming
Help me
Draw me close
Neck to chest
Breast to sheer lushness
Help me
Melt with me
Dissolve into my oasis
Let's face this passion that
Swells and swallows
All of our todays and tomorrows
Within this love we share
Slowly take me there
Where thighs quake
Skin bakes
Inhibition break

(cont.)

My love
Come near to me
Breath to breath
Tongue --tip to tip
Lip to lip
We sip holy nectar
High from this rhapsody trip
To the land of orgasmic
Fantastic spasms
That out last this life
Come near me
I need to be near you

I'M SORRY

The words came as flying bullets
Blindly aiming
Desiring to maim you any way I could
They came
Filled with hurt
Stabbing with pain
Spitting evil
Wanting to destroy you whole
I could not control them
Once they moved my bowels
Rushed through my throat
And vomited all the ill feelings bottled up inside
I'm sorry
I didn't mean all the things I meant
But should not have said
Forgive me
Please
Forgive me

GONE

I want to weep
Fall to the earth
Beat my fist on dusty breasts
Dig my nails into grassy flesh
I want to wail
Belt out bellowing water
Flood the world with my sorrow
Vomit tears upon oceans of dreams
I want to cry
Rip the soul from my eyes
Banish my spirit to Sheol
No soul will this body hold
I want to yell
Yell! Yell! Yell!
Appeal to God to overturn his verdict
Beg the heavenly hosts
To give him back to me
I blubber
Ingesting snot
Drinking tears
Regurgitating moans
Howling madness
A banshee of sadness
Yet he's still gone
His ears immune to my screams
Heart hardened against my whimpers
He is gone
Gone
Gone
Forever gone

(cont...)

To the place where I banished him for all times
Now I rock to the rhythm of my foolish sniffling
Mewling melancholy melodies
When all he wished to be
Was mine...

ONE SEPTEMBER NIGHT

The spark started late one night over carrot cake
Your fork to my lips
Cream on my tongue
Smile on your face
Our eyes locked

My soul pulled towards you
I tried to swallow it down but
My heart drifted to thoughts inconceivable
You and me! Unbelievable
Yet I now believe

My eyes drifted to paintings of erotic fruit
Sticky pistols, juicy apples, dark pit peaches
As my erotic fruit ripened frighteningly
I tried to clear my mind of this dangerous chemistry

Yet it lingered
And I lingered close to your mouth
Pretending to grasp every word
But it was your lips I desired
hoping to brush them
To touch them
To taste them
But...

We walked back into the late summer air
Hugged a little too tight
Hips pressed close

(cont...)

Hearts competing in alternating pumps
Our lips whispering weak goodbyes
Tried hard to avoid one another's eyes
Unbeknownst of what was to come

And now
yearning still

DRUMMER BOY

you and me
unlikely
yet I'm intoxicated by your youth
the smoothness of your skin
soft like baby blue
sweet like honey dew
I smile at the glint of innocence in your eyes
you are man
full grown
yet a child in things known and unknown
it's clear God lives in you
although you kick and scream
curse and blaspheme
the Lord has you
and you cannot escape
the Church is your fate
destined to moan and spit
howl prophesies from the pulpit
oh! rebel lover – friend - brother
enigmatic fantastic druid of musical magic
I'm impressed by your dreams
yet I withdraw from your scene
I'm not a part of your world
just an illusion
a phantom of delusion
enjoying you on borrowed time
tomorrow I'll fade to dark
and you will be a figment of memory
drumming specter of fantasy

DIRTY MIND

The anticipation alone triggers dangerous warmth
within my love pot
I clench my thighs and close my eyes as I drop hot
volcanic honey
Glazing my most scared spot - the creator of
queendoms, the holy grail of Camelot
Glossing lips begging to be kissed
Oh! Forget me not!
They pucker in wanton bliss, pulsating in frenzy
Swelling into a silken temptress
My imagination plots to keep you close
As you trot down corridors of my psyche to find me
waiting
Anticipating your key to enter my slot- to turn, to
click, to probe, to unlock
Every inhibition I got until my flesh rots into earth
Then like the first of spring, I'll rebirth
Orgasmically convert into worship of your heavenly
insert
We transform from human to beast gorging in a
carnal feast
I crave for you to find the spot that tames this
lioness of mine, that trains my savage kind
To purr nonstop like a divine feline upon an
Egyptian pedestal fine
Yet I forgot to forget to watch the clock
As my mind count down the time
To love you lots

LOVE SPELL

I fancy you like changing leaves.
Fire tipped and screaming in the breeze;
beautifully dangling like a busty tease.
I fancy you like changing leaves.

I reach for you like floating dreams
vanishing with the first sunbeams
lingering between realms and scenes.
I reach for you like floating dreams.

I dance for you with arched foot.
Uprooting lilies with each toe put.
Twirling earth making fairy dust from soot.
I dance for you with arched foot.

I enchant you with mystical brew.
Bewitch with hips wrapped in violet blue.
Enthrall with kisses as wet as morning dew.
I enchant you with mystical brew.

I fancy. I reach. I dance. I enchant.
Give me infinity. Damn can't!
Your seed of love, in my bosom implant.
Now your heart to me you will grant.

NO MORE
Like emerald grass under the scorching sun
Brown and burned by the heat of life
Pressed down by feet
Pressured and ground in the ground
Once beautiful now gone
Dead little shadow of what was
But can not be again
Faded into gold then deathly tan
A blade—cut and broken
No more...

FOREVER
the concrete is hot beneath my feet
cracked heels dry and peeling
forced to dance upon the heat
it hurts but the sun is so sweet
I laugh
teeth parted
tongue shining
my throat sings
as we walk hand and hand
you shaking your head calling me country
barefoot on New York City
I skip beneath skyscrapers

we were so happy then
love was our daily bread
passion our shelter from the rain
that was before the years
killed our fantastic romantic antics
but love survived
and we are
and will always be
forever

REBORN INTO PURE

How did I get here?
Dimension of the confused
I've been stripped of my robes
Crown ripped from my brow
Scepter smashed
Throne crushed
The command of my mouth ignored
I am nothing
A common peasant girl
With wiry hair
Sun burned skin
Tattered and torn garments
Virtue gave me my riches
Vulgarity stripped them away
I have shamed my clan
Off with my head!
The enemy pillaging the coffer
Between my legs
Impure daughter of the Most High
Idol worshipping self
Pleasure--Desire
Take this flesh and nail it to a tree
Whip the devil out of me
Bleed these wicked veins
Bury this body in soft earth
Soft enough so I can emerge
Like a butterfly
Renewed
Brand new
reborn into pure

LETTING GO

My eyes refuse to tear
Tears evaporate into diamond dust
Highlighting my quivering cheeks
I breathe in
My chest hurts
My heart, a lame organ beating sluggishly
Pumping slovenly
Blue with thoughts of you
My fists tight
Knuckles ache
I try to pull you close to me
But the resistance is too great
One hand lets go
Fingers raw and bent backwards
Memories invade my mind
Shadows of happy times pas de bouree
Through my thoughts
A smile bends these lips
Frozen downward—cracking my solemn face
Hardened by the hurts you hurled at me
Yet my grip is strong
My elbows red—joints swollen
You pull—pull—yank away
But I want you close to me
I can't forget what it felt like in your arms
Adrenaline grants me one last pull
Yet I snap
My heart fails
My body is weary
My bones break under your alienation of affection

(cont...)

I give up
Fall to the earth a puddle of flesh
And
Let go

NUMB
There is nothing
An echoing emptiness in my chest
My eyes so dry and hurt
Focus unfocused
Thoughts unthinkable
I sit
Sleep
Wake
Eat
Sit
Sleep
Wake
Eat
Still
There is nothing

I STILL LOVE YOU

Your level of perfection has plummeted
All too human you have become
I no longer see your divinity
Yet you are still the one
Who makes me promise forever
You have fallen to earth
Your wings incinerated
Your halo shattered
Your pedestal crumbled beneath you
Oh, earthling, my king
I still love you
I've seen your fatal flaw
Your Achilles heel
Your tender spot
The crack in your armor
Your mortality exposed
Yet you are mine
And I treasure you
Be not ashamed of your weaknesses
Do not hang your head to the ground
Sleep well my common man
For you are all my desires met
And I still love you

MURDERER

I've done the unthinkable
Womb and heart empty
Both bleeding desperation
I died too
Make no mistake
The soul has left this body
Its destination unknown
A zombie I am
Begging for rebirth
To not be aborted
And left to rot in this world

ETERNITY IS THE BEST WE CAN DO

Who are we?
Great lovers pulled asunder
By life's damnable dilemmas
We ache
Hearts smooshed like champagne grapes
Pounded until streams bleeding red
Once upon a time
I was yours and you were mine
But now possession is uncertain
For our obsession with teaching
Each other lessons
Has become our first love
We promised forever
Forever seemed like a minute
Now the thought of it is a mighty long time
Fallen from grace
No longer divine
But profane in commitment and pain
How oh Lord did this great love diminish
Into a sorry hard hearted finish?
Or is this just the interim
A bad break with morals to take
A booster for our next resurrection—renaissance
A launch into a greater love
Than what we had once
You and I
I and you
Eternity is the best we can do!

LAMENTATION
What is this life
But brief days
Expiring quickly
We search for you
For purpose
Yet it all seems worthless
For we know nothing the more we know
Oh Lord!
Hear my lament
I would pull the skin from my bones
And dance around flames
If only you would whisper your name
In my ears
So I can hear
And know you are not deaf
Oh Death
Haunts us all
A haint that
Hovers over us day by day
Beckoning us to come his way
I beg you life
Life
Life
Eternal
Life upon this earth
Without a vampire bite
Just eternal life
Oh Rock of Ancient Days!
Hide not the tree from me!
I crave to feast on its fruit

(cont...)

So infinity I will see
Hear me
Heal me
Hear me!

I AM SUFFOCATING

My spirit is much too tender
Like a sapling with new life
Yet my young days seem old
Withered within my youth
A baby donning wrinkles
Fresh leather with deep creases
The disappointment of beautiful life
Chokes me with firm hands
Fingers that lock tight without mercy
Nails that scrape flesh
Thumbs that press throats
I gasp but no air
No air
No air
I falter and struggle
Kiss the lips of those who slay me
I bite tenderly—stinging with affection
Lick playfully desiring compassion
Sucking soft flesh praying to inhale a free breath
But no air
No breath for this body bubbling boastfully with
creativity
Streaming with color
Vibrant and vivid with light
Yet the darkness haunts me
And my life leaves me
Weeping
Weeping
I am suffocating

BLAME GAME
You stole my heart with poetry
Seduced me with a lie
Fondled me with imagery
Tickled me with rhyme
Made love to me with your pen
Splattered me in ink
Tore me like paper from end to end
A wordless heap into the trash I sink

THOSE EYES

At a glance my inward parts quake
Tremble to the beat of my heart
Rumble in scarlet fits
That highlight these cheeks that glow at you
My breath sits still upon my lips
Afraid to leave for fear it's the last
I hide behind a smile
Too afraid to peek into those eyes
Those eyes that seem to see me
See deep into all I am
One stare
I am rendered helpless
Made weakling—frail and open hearted
Exposed—nude—soul naked
Bucking against the intensity of your gaze
Yet
Without intention I look up
And become captivated by those orbs of life
My heart falls prostrate at your feet
And I melt
Within those eyes

CHANGES

Never did I see the end coming
I yelled goodbye with false conviction
I prayed you away with a
Heart hoping that God could not hear
Now I know the end is near
Over a decade it has been you and me
Tumbling between love and despair
Holding hands and tripping feet
Kissing lips while biting tongues
But never did I fear the end
I thought death would separate us
But death came during life
Shadowed in broken hearts
Shattered trust
Misused funds
And misplaced lust
Now we are here
The unbreakable broken
A great oak with gnarled roots
And rotten branches
Yet I love you still
But the pain of it all
Swallows me like Jonah
Instead of being vomited up
I've been crapped out
Now all I desire is to be clean
Washed clean of you
Scrubbed brand new
Now my only fear is tomorrow
The intricate horror of life without Latif

YOU

My chest hurts when I think of you
Warm pressure cramps my heart
The idea of you warms my thighs
Dampen my sacred parts
Oh you!
Who has mysteriously appeared to me
Lifting my sorrow bent head
Forcing smiles upon me
Painting love upon my belly
Can you be who
My soul has searched for through the ages
The imaginary figure my pen has prophesized about
The object of my poetic affection comes to life
You
You who snatch my breath when your eyes meet
mine
Who sing of undying admiration
Who unfold soul mate revelations
Lulling me to sleep with hot fingers
Tantalizing tongue
Passionate intermingling parts
How did you sneak into my heart
Creep into the caution locked corridor of my every
desire
You!
Oh you!
It seems as if we were before
Before this life began
As if we were always
Although I can't recall when

(cont...)

But I knew you before I knew you
And I craved you
Before we traded nectar for cream
You
Sweet innovative you
Could you be the man of my dreams?

UNTITLED
You linger on my shoulder
Like the moon in the daytime sky
Fading into the backdrop
Like an envious evil eye
Staring into the silence
Counting time like grains of sand
Dropping each grain in your gnarled palms
Anticipating my demise
But baby
I'm untouchable
Impalpable
Invincible
So move on and haunt someone who cares

INCOMPLETE THOUGHT

It has been a long time since I've been plucked
—my stem preened
—my leaves spread
—my pistol made wet, slick, and sloppy
Sticky by your sweet nectar
Oh!
My bloom is wide and ready
Bury your face into my flower
—inhale
—enjoy
—become inebriated by my scent
Pollinate my fertile center
Enter delicately without hesitancy
Implant
Enchant
Un-plant this soil moist and ready for….

WHAT HAPPENED TO SACRED SEXUALITY?
Divine female bodies intertwining with masculinity
Grinding fairy dust into diamonds
With every touch
Each magical thrust
Holy orgasmic blood rush
To sacred parts soaked with love
Dripping with lust
What happened?
Oh, fallen one—promiscuous angel
Halo handcuffing you from bed to bed
Soulless shell and vacant eyes
Writhing back and wide spread thighs
Vomiting up truth and swallowing lies
All your self worth pulsating from between your legs
Cold damp funk clouding your heart and head
Emotionally dead
Lady of golden sand dunes
Glistening mahogany or
Black shadow of moon
Morally decayed
Your spark dying within a bodily tomb of flesh
An empty hole filled with random poles
Traded and pounded
Raided and forgotten
Lady left cold
With semen soaked lips burning holes through your
soul
Drunk off of false liberation
Stomach filled with swimming libation
Drowned and choking on low self esteem

(cont...)

Slave of male fantasies
Setting your panties free
Reeking in desperation
Submitting to degradation, bisexuality and pimp
manipulation
Oh worthless woman full of so much worth!
Bowing in worship of phallic beams
Thighs sticky and stinking of virile creams
Beauty queen oblivious to your beauty
Trapped within her own echoing screams
But nothing is the way it seems
When you are a black girl lost...

SECRETS

Little minions
Perched upon my knees
pawing my shoulders
Clinging to my hair
Hugging my feet
They follow me
Grinning creatures of darkness
Transparent shadows
Dancing down my back
Set me free!
Monstrous lot!
They laugh and tickle my ribs
For they know my pride dare not cast them away
My ego will house them for infinity
Like fungus on a tree
They are a part of me

I WAS DEAD
Dry bones baking in the wilderness
Ashes and dust twirling into quiet
Then you came
Your presence a prayer
A whisper provoking God to breath on me
And The Spirit moved over the chaos of my soul
And there was light
My eyes opened to greet your divine kiss—heavily
sigh
My spirit was renewed
The darkness fell away
As I fell into your arms
Thank you for loving me Ari

CLUB
The music vibrated through us
As the crowd swayed like palms
We danced and our sweat mingled
Mingled and joined in musky salty rivers
We danced and our hearts pounded
The rhythm seduced our hips
We pumped in clothes
Damp and sticky
But we loved the groovy dew
We danced like no tomorrow
Then your hand slipped down my skirt
My pelvis pumped against your fondling finger
That forced my love to squirt
I moaned beneath the laughing crowd
– drunk and living free
We danced as I achieved climax
We danced
Just you and me

DIVORCE
like emerald grass
under the scorching sun
brown and burned
by the heat of life
pressed down
by feet
pressured and grinded
in the ground
once beautiful
now gone
dead little shadow
of what was
but not to be again
faded into gold
then deathly tan
a blade
cut and broken
no more

ALL THE WORDS HAVE BEEN USED
vainly describing misdiagnosed emotions
I have waxed poetic about
him and him
not knowing I would ever find you
now I have
but there is nothing left to say
I won't coo about your eyes
fawn over your lips
force my heart to palpitate on paper
reminiscing on our late night loving
I have done all that!
filled books with empty words
and pretty images
idealistic fantasies of love and lust
dreams of ardor personified
and all of my masculine muses
fell short of my expectations
so with you I will live the poem
I will be the words
you, the paper
life, the pen

UNTIL MORNING
let's make our life in this cushioned bosom
where we close our eyes to dream
let's slip under silken blouse and lie our heads on
fluffy breast
as we tangle beneath the windmill that dangles
gleefully
from our sheetrock sky
baby let's share skin
as we wrestle within the folds of heartbeats
paint roses across our cheeks with naughty
whispers
let's live life within this airy sleep
and just love
love
love
Until morning

WHERE'S POETRY?
You left me when happiness came
It aroused you when I wallowed in pain
Back then you flowed heavily
Like fibroid pressured scarlet drip
Now you lay low
Wordless and silent
Forcing me to scribble empty words
Wasting ink
Squandering time
Trying to woo you back into my hand
I beg you to kiss my fingertips
Tickle me with fancy words
Sensual imagery
Holy insight
Lava hot emotion
Just come back to me
My first love
My true lover
Satiate me again
And again
And again
Please…

I AWAIT YOU
my love
Child of my prime
Surprising life dwelling inside
I await you happily
Completing my trinity
Of love
I await you
With breath abated
Heart open
Arms ajar
Soul seeking your likeness
Oh daughter!
Divine female presented
To me
I await you
Anticipate you
See you soon

REMEMBERING
Fragments of you and me
Happy
Free
Unconquerable
Yet
All an illusion
Invisible odds growing gigantic
Killing all the romantic
Fragments
Of
my memories
Of
You and me

THERE ARE NO WORDS

Poets are silenced
Their hands tremble
Pens fall
There are no words
No words at all to describe our love
No phrase birthed or aborted
Through infinity
That illustrates the phenomenon
Of you and me
Divinity exudes through our union
Infinite communion
Partaking of love
Drunken with lust
Dripping with like
Engorged with trust
Quaking thrusts of passionate us
There are no words
No words at all

RUAH
Spirit
Breath
Wind
Beautiful child
Golden and new
Molded from true love
Created within the folds of my craving heart
You came to me in sweet surprise
Each day I surrender to your toothless smile
And thank the great "I AM"
For blessing me once again
With a soul I don't deserve
I adore you-
You complete me-
Ruah
You have breathed new life into me
The breeze of your breath has
Given my spirit new health
And I love you
Forever
Little girl of mine

THE CYCLE
all children are born in Eden
innocent
naked
happy
free
ignorant of good and evil
until
serpentine parents offer apples of knowledge
fruits of fruitless society
and us babies gobble them up
expecting
infinite life
sacred understanding
but those apples of good intentions
are always tinged with doom
the descent from divinity begins
and we all fall
fall
fall
we all
go
tumbling down

I DANCE
I dance
Naked
Hips rotating
Turning breezes into tornadoes
Balancing on tip toe
I leap into the callus sun
Skin warmed by its flaming embrace upon my face
I dance
Echoing claps
My wings flap as I twirl
Twist
Whirl
Shimmy with joy
Enveloped in this wondrous world
I dance
Yes I dance
I love this live
This blessed life
Life is a hallowed thing

WAITING FOR YOU

Stinky sweet sheets
Soaked with you and me
Wrapped around twisting torsos
Trembling for me for you
Your love is...
Oh...oh...oh...oh...ah...ah...ah...
All I need
Between these hugging thighs and craving eyes
I miss you
I need you
I want you
It has been a night or two
And I am
A torn-tangled-mangled
Lusting lump of woman
Waiting
Waiting
Waiting for you

TO ARI
When the trees dress in skirts of fire
The cool breath of Mother Nature tickles my neck
I dream of cozy cuddles beneath silken blankets
Tucked deep within the folds of your arms
I fall into honey Autumn thoughts and revel on
How sweet it is to be loved by you